Original title:
Island Secrets

Copyright © 2025 Creative Arts Management OÜ
All rights reserved.

Author: Hugo Fitzgerald
ISBN HARDBACK: 978-1-80581-540-2
ISBN PAPERBACK: 978-1-80581-067-4
ISBN EBOOK: 978-1-80581-540-2

Cradle of Moonlit Wonders

Under the stars, we dance and sway,
Laughter echoes, chasing dark away.
A crab with a grin just stole my shoe,
While fish in tuxedos swim past, too!

The seaweed wiggles, it tickles our toes,
We chase the waves in extravagant clothes.
The moon whispers secrets in silvery tones,
As we dig for treasure, just shells and bones.

The Forgotten Tide's Lament

Once a wave wearing a top hat tried,
To dance with a starfish, but they both cried.
The tide came in, with a splash and a wink,
Pulling the surfboard; we spilled our drink!

The gulls gathered round for a slightly weird show,
As we juggled coconuts in a row.
But the tide had plans, it yanked us away,
And all we got back were our jokes on display!

Stories Etched in Sand

In the sand, we carve our mightiest fears,
A mermaid's diary, and surfboard jeers.
With each crashing wave, our secrets unwind,
And flip-flops giggle, they're one of a kind!

The seagulls peek in, stealing tales that we tell,
About the treasures hidden with shells in a shell.
With a twist of our fate, and a splash of the foam,
We find our lost laughter—together, we roam!

The Veil of Ocean Mysteries

Beneath the surface, the fish hold a feast,
With jellybeans swimming—oh, what a beast!
A dolphin jokes, with a wink and a flip,
While octopuses plot their next wild trip!

The secrets of seaweed pull at our hair,
We gather in circles, plotting our dare.
Tales of lost socks and treasure so grand,
Make waves of laughter across the warm sand!

The Whispers of Distant Shoals

In waters deep, the fish all chat,
About a crab that wore a hat.
They giggle and they flip with glee,
While seahorses dance, wild and free.

A sunken treasure chest sits tight,
Filled with shells that gleam so bright.
The otters launch a game of catch,
With pearls they found—a clever batch!

The Tides that Remember

The waves tell tales of days gone by,
Of dolphins that wore ties so spry.
They surf beneath the moonlit beams,
While seagulls plot their wacky schemes.

Old clam shells snap, a loud debate,
"Who's got more pearls?" they loudly state.
The crabs just chuckle, pinch and play,
In this odd world, they run the day.

A Journey to Hidden Pastures

On grassy hills where goats can sing,
They munch on leaves and wear a ring.
A parrot squawks, "Join in the fun!"
As turtles dance—oh what a run!

The rumors say of cheese so rare,
Hidden beneath that coconut hair.
They plan a feast with fruit galore,
"A picnic here? We all want more!"

The Scribes of Forgotten Shores

Upon the sand, the crabs do write,
In tiny scripts, both bold and light.
They ink their tales with jellyfish,
Of a sneaky whale who grants a wish!

The gulls conspire with old sea rooks,
Sharing tales like clever books.
With each new tide, the stories swell,
Of wacky beachside stories to tell!

Echoes of Lost Time

In the sand, a flip-flop lies,
A crab steals it with hungry eyes,
The sun laughs, the waves agree,
Who knew footwear was so funny?

Lanterns Over the Distant Horizon

A lantern glows on a wobbly dock,
Fishermen dance, they can't quite walk,
Fish cackle as they slip away,
They've heard this joke, 'It's a catch today!'

Salted Memories in Driftwood

Driftwood whispers to seashells fair,
Telling tales of salty air,
While seagulls squawk out punchlines bold,
Laughter echoing, never old.

The Caves of Conch Harmony

In conch caves, a band plays loud,
With shells and seaweed, they draw a crowd,
A sea breeze notes each silly tune,
While fish shimmy under the moon.

The Lure of Crystal Waters

In sunny spots where shadows play,
The fish wear hats, and dolphins sway.
With a splash and a giggle loud,
A turtle joins the frolic crowd.

Behold the crabs that dance so spry,
With tiny ties and a winked eye.
They throw a party on the shore,
Where seaweed snacks are never poor.

Whispers from the Sea Glass

Old bottles float with tales to tell,
Of jellyfish that ring a bell.
They gossip low about a whale,
Whose jokes are large, but never stale.

The sandcastles wear crowns of foam,
As seagulls chirp a silly poem.
Each wave brings tidings from the deep,
Where mermaids laugh and dolphins leap.

Dancers Beneath the Wave

An octopus can really dance,
With eight-armed moves that make you prance.
The starfish claps with all its might,
While squids put on a flashy light.

Under the sea, they take the stage,
With bubbles popping, all the rage.
They twirl and swirl in pure delight,
As fish throw snacks for appetite.

The Call of the Siren's Isle

On a breeze the laughter flies,
As mermaids lure with playful sighs.
They promise treasures, but beware,
For seaweed wigs are their snare!

The shells hold secrets in their grip,
Of sea foam drinks and giddy trips.
Catch a wave, or take a chance,
In salty whims, we all shall prance.

The Cradle of the Turquoise Cove

In the cove where laughter flows,
Seashells wear a fancy pose,
Crabs dance like they know the beat,
While starfish think they're oh-so-sweet.

Waves tickle toes, a cheeky tease,
Cocktail umbrellas sway with ease,
Seagulls squawk a silly tune,
Under the watchful eye of the moon.

Turtles drop in for a drink,
Join the party, don't you think?
With fish in sunglasses, bright and bold,
Each moment here feels like pure gold.

Watch out for that sneaky wave,
It's got secrets, but we're brave,
In this cove of mirth and play,
Life's a splash, come join the fray!

An Oath to the Ocean's Depths

We pledge our hearts to bubbles bright,
To seaweed dances, oh what a sight!
Jellyfish juggle in the deep,
While playful dolphins laugh and leap.

Who knew the ocean's got such flair,
With fishy friends that love to share?
Octopuses in top hats prance,
While clowns in coral lead the dance.

Manta rays glide like they own the show,
Teaching us how to safely row,
As kelp forests sway, we sing,
To the rhythm of waves, our giggles ring.

A toast to tides that tickle and tease,
Here's to the foam and salty breeze,
Together with laughter, we take the leap,
In these depths, the secrets we keep!

The Light that Guides the Lost

A beacon shines from rocky face,
With winking light, it sets the pace,
For ships that wobble, nearly sway,
It's guiding all who've lost their way.

They say it's magic, a whimsical spark,
That draws in sailors with a heart full of lark,
As gulls mimic sirens, crisp and clear,
Whispering wishes into the ear.

But watch for the fog, it's sneaky and sly,
It clouds your path like a well-timed lie,
And mermaids giggle, oh so aloof,
While you swim circles, under the hoof.

So cherish that light, twinkling above,
It's a lighthouse of laughter, filled with love,
For every lost soul that asks for direction,
Find their way home through smiles and reflection!

Portals to Ancient Waters

Beneath the waves, a door swings wide,
To realms of laughter where fish confide,
Each ripple whispers tales untold,
As clams and crabs share secrets old.

Octopi paint with colors bright,
Creating murals in the twilight,
Whales play hide and seek with glee,
In a watery wonderland, wild and free.

With every splash, a giggle rings,
As mermaids show off their bling-bling,
Turtles dressed for a soirée dance,
Inviting all to join the prance.

So dive with joy into these depths,
Where laughter glows and sorrow steps,
In portals vast, both strange and sweet,
Adventure awaits with laughter's beat!

Stories Carved in Coral

A crab wore glasses, quite absurd,
He read the tides like a silly bird.
Whispers in the shells spoke of delight,
As dolphins giggled, frolicking in light.

Treasure chests full of seaweed snacks,
Jellyfish jived on the ocean tracks.
A parrot inspired with a song so bright,
Claimed seahorses danced every night.

The octopus painted with colors bold,
While starfish swapped secrets, tales untold.
Mermaids laughed at their tangled hair,
As lobsters waltzed without a care.

At sunset's glow, the party would start,
With sand dollars joining in, that's the art!
Crabs threw confetti from the sand so fine,
Celebrating life with a splash of brine.

Beneath a Sky of Starry Dreams

A fish wore a crown and ruled the bay,
With a court of clams that knew how to play.
Under the moon, they held a ball,
With seaweed streamers lined up in a hall.

A turtle DJ spun the tunes so loud,
While shrimps formed a crowd and danced unbowed.
Oysters giggled as they polished their pearls,
As popcorn bubbles swirled in twirls.

A starfish rare told jokes with flair,
While pufferfish puffed up without a care.
Whales sang ballads, deep and sincere,
As everyone laughed, their worries disappeared.

A night like this, they'd dream and sway,
Where silliness bloomed in a gleeful display.
Under starry skies with a sparkling gleam,
Life's just a dream beneath beams of beam.

The Lighthouse Keeper's Tale

A keeper of light with a quirky pitch,
Made seagulls laugh with a fountain of quips.
Every evening his job was a lark,
While the lighthouse blinked with a wink and a spark.

He counted waves like kids count sheep,
With a bucket of clams, his secrets to keep.
Old barnacles told tales from the deep,
While foghorns hummed a tune, not too cheap.

One day a pirate knocked on his door,
Claiming to hear the lighthouse's roar.
"Can I trade you some gold for a snack?"
The keeper replied, "Just shower with clams, Jack!"

They shared a laugh beneath the moon,
As seagulls squawked a silly tune.
In the lighthouse, tales spread wide and tall,
Who knew a beacon could be such a ball?

Cradled by the Ocean's Breath

A whale painted graffiti on the rocks,
While sea turtles debated over socks.
Octopuses brewed seawater tea,
Chortling with laughter, so blissfully free.

Crabs in bow ties danced in a line,
Inviting all fish to savor the brine.
Underwater parties, oh what a sight!
As anemones twirled in the shimmering light.

Fiddler crabs strutted with swagger and flair,
Shells painted bright, they were quite the pair.
Whispering mermaids with laughter like bells,
Spilled guffaws that rang through the swells.

With clinking of shells and a joyful cheer,
The ocean embraced, always near.
In the waves, joy spun like a thread,
A place where adventure was joyously bred.

The Echo of Shells in Twilight

In twilight's glow, shells start to sing,
With whispers of crabs, they dance in a ring.
A starfish on stage, it winks and it sways,
While seagulls take bets on the best of their plays.

The tide rolls in, with laughter and cheer,
While fish crack a joke, it's all in good spirit.
"Why did the clam refuse to take a seat?"
It said, "I'm too shellfish, it's just too neat!"

So gather the sands, let's start a new game,
As the sun bows down, lighting the world's flame.
With giggles of dolphins, they leap through the night,
Echoes of joy in this watery site.

The Enigma of Wave-Tossed Memories

Waves toss around tales that tickle the mind,
With memories dancing like seaweed entwined.
A fish with a monocle, reading a book,
Who knew fish had stories? Oh, come take a look!

A crab in a tux, he's ready to prance,
While jellyfish giggle in a shimmery trance.
"Why don't we ever see octopus play?"
It's too busy hiding—now where did it stray?

The ocean's a riddle that keeps us bewitched,
With secrets so silly, and walls that are stitched.
As starfish practice for their big Broadway show,
We're here for the laughs, let the fun overflow!

Secrets Beneath the Blue Horizon

Beneath the blue vastness, where sea turtles glide,
A treasure chest laughs, oh what secrets it hides!
With pearls dressed like snowflakes at fancy soirées,
While fish gather round, gossiping in arrays.

"Did you hear the news?" a whale starts to hum,
"An octopus just scored a date with a drum!"
With bubbles that burst, and laughter galore,
The ocean's a stage, who could ask for more?

Each wave brings a chuckle, a splash and a tease,
As dolphins spin tales on their tippy-toes, please!
The horizon's a puzzle that sparkles and beams,
With funny little secrets wrapped up in our dreams.

The Dreams of the Serene Sea

The serene sea hums, with dreams so absurd,
Where fish form a band and the seaweed's a bird.
They play with the waves, in a comical whirl,
As seashells clap hands in a watery twirl.

A rogue little squid paints the ocean deep blue,
While crabs join the chorus, singing loud too.
"Why are seagulls so good at their game?"
"Because they're always winging it, it's never the same!"

So let the waves dance, let the stories unfold,
Each bubble a laugh, each splash turns to gold.
In the dreams of the sea, let's play just right,
As the stars start to twinkle, and sleep holds us tight.

Beneath the Mango Trees

Gather 'round the mango trees,
Where squirrels plot their silly heists.
A banana peel, a coconut breeze,
Who knew fruits could start such feasts?

The monkeys dance with reckless flair,
Wearing hats made from bright old leaves.
They jest about the humans near,
Who can't catch them, how hard they grieve!

A tourist drops her picnic treat,
A sandwich flies, it's quite the show!
The mangoes chuckle, a juicy feat,
As they watch the comical flow!

Underneath those leafy crowns,
Life's a circus case of glee.
You'd laugh out loud, you'd never frown,
In the shade of the mango tree.

Lurking Between the Waves

Oh, the fish with shades and flair,
Surfing 'round with plenty of style.
They giggle at divers unaware,
Whose bubbles burst and cause a smile.

A crab with an attitude bold,
Waves its claws in a funny dance.
It thinks he's worth more than gold,
Sassy in his little prance.

Seagulls squawk, making a fuss,
Dropping shells like they own the day.
Amidst the waves, you'll find a bus,
Of dolphins who just love to play!

With secrets swirling 'neath the sea,
There's laughter bubbling like champagne.
The ocean whispers, joy is free,
In this watery, wild domain!

The Tide's Silent Confession

The tide rolls in with a silly grin,
Tickling toes as it retreats.
It whispers secrets with a spin,
Only to return with playful beats.

Resting on the shore, it claims,
Every shell a tiny tale.
Those beach towels, oh what a shame,
They're tangled up, a true travail!

Lone flip-flop wanders about,
Searching for its sandal mate.
Together they'd dance without doubt,
But tides keep changing their fate.

As sun sets low, the waves sigh loud,
A silent confession, so absurd.
Taking tips from the evening cloud,
Shall we laugh at what we've heard?

Shadows of the Coral Reef

In the coral, shadows play,
Creatures hiding, just for fun.
Anemones sway in a ballet,
With fish that zoom, oh what a run!

The parrotfish in disco hues,
Sporting smiles as bright as day.
They gossip softly, share the news,
Of the octopus's recent play!

A clam clamors for a spot on stage,
But shrimps are quick to steal the light.
Oh, the antics of each cage,
Make the underwater world feel right.

Between the colors, laughter flows,
Who knew reefs had such a flair?
With frolicsome moods that ebbs and glows,
The secrets of the deep, laid bare!

When the Tides Hold Their Breath

When waves pause in a silly dance,
The fish wear hats and take a chance.
They juggle seashells, laugh and slip,
While crabs tap toes, get ready to flip.

The sun rolls over, giggling loud,
As seagulls dive in, joining the crowd.
A sailor's hat on a dolphin's snout,
Who knew the sea could prance about?

Sandcastles wobble, quite the sight,
As mermaids gossip 'til the night.
They trade tall tales of jellyfish,
Who swam in circles, dreaming of fish.

And when the tides finally let go,
The sea spills secrets, setting the show.
The beach holds laughter, crisp and grand,
As tides breathe easy, on warm sand.

The Ghostlight on the Horizon

A flicker glows where waves do peek,
Is it a ghost? Or just a cheek?
The crabs all stare with sparked delight,
As glowworms dance, out of sheer fright.

A pirate's hat stuck on a tree,
Claims it's a treasure, come see with me!
But all that's found are shoes and socks,
And a rubber duck in a big box.

The moon whispers jokes to the tide,
As fish line up, they swim with pride.
They wink at boats with silly names,
Like "Silly Sally" and "Captain Games."

The light glows brighter, what a tease,
Turns out it's just a fancy breeze.
With chuckles echoing far and wide,
The ghostlight ends their laughing ride.

Whispers of the Tidal Breeze

A breeze comes in, with tickles and sighs,
It tells tall tales, under sunny skies.
The seagulls gather, their beaks in a row,
To hear the gossip that breezes throw.

"Oh did you hear what the crab just said?
He found a lost sock in his cozy bed!"
The clams chuckle, "Now that's just bizarre,
Bet the sock thinks it's a big ol' star!"

Waves giggle softly, in rippling tones,
As dolphins dance, on their slippery bones.
With flips and tricks, they mimic the breeze,
Creating laughter with utmost ease.

The tide holds secrets in every swirl,
As fish throw confetti, watch them unfurl.
The whispers travel, from sea to shore,
A funny tale, who could ask for more?

Shadows Beneath the Coconut Grove

In the shadows of trees, the coconuts sway,
A parrot squawks jokes, brightening the day.
He swings on branches, with bellyache laughs,
At the sight of crabs in lovely green scarves.

The breeze carries whispers from leaf to leaf,
Monkey swings in, with a tale of mischief.
He swung too hard and lost his grip,
Now he only wears his favorite flip.

Laughter echoes as shadows entwine,
With secrets and giggles, sweet and divine.
A treasure map drawn in the sand,
Points to a picnic; it's quite unmanned.

Coconuts drop, causing bursts of cheer,
Is it a party? Why, yes, my dear!
With fruits and fun, as dusk starts to show,
In the shadows, laughter just seems to grow.

Whispers Beneath the Palms

Beneath the palms where laughter sways,
Sneaky crabs plot their funny plays.
A coconut fell with a thud and a crack,
The parrot squawked, 'Hey, there's a snack!'

The sunburnt tourists dance with glee,
While seagulls steal their fries with glee.
Flip-flops flying in a wild parade,
A beach ball bouncing, dreams are made!

The tide rolls in with a playful cheer,
A splash on the shoes, oh dear, oh dear!
Sandcastles crumble in grand delight,
"Who built that one?" "Not me, not quite!"

So gather near where shadows play,
With funny tales to brighten the day.
Under the palms, let secrets fly,
In this sunny place, we laugh and sigh.

The Hidden Tide

When waves whisper tales of long ago,
The fishermen smile with a cheeky glow.
They chuckle low at the seaweed's dance,
'Is that a mermaid? Just my pants!'

The fish here gossip, or so they think,
"Catch me if you can, I'm faster than ink!"
Hooks and lines tangled in a mess,
"Let's have a splashing contest, more or less!"

Turtles in shades lounge with pride,
While dolphins giggle, "Come take a ride!"
Shells with stories, all lined in a row,
"Did you hear about the crab called Joe?"

The tide rolls back, a breezy tease,
Leaving behind laughter on the breeze.
Oh, what fun in this watery game,
In the splash and the giggle, nothing's the same!

Sheltered Dunes and Silent Echoes

The dunes hide secrets, or so they say,
With every breeze, they sweep them away.
A lost flip-flop tells tales of a run,
'Hey, wait for me, I'm not done for fun!'

Sandcastles built with the grandest care,
A tide arrives with a splash and a stare.
"Oops!" yells a kid, as it washes away,
"Let's build again, we've got all day!"

Under the sun, a sunburnt crab grins,
Chasing seagulls as the laughter begins.
Silent echoes of giggles abound,
As shells laugh at the silliness found.

Through whispered winds, the jokes we share,
In nature's comedy, life's a fair.
So come build laughter beneath the sun,
In the shelter of dunes, we all have fun!

Mysteries of the Forgotten Cove

In a cove forgotten by time and tide,
The treasure is laughter that we can't hide.
A pirate's hat floats, way up on high,
"Take me to your leader," the gulls slyly cry.

Seaweed wigs on the fish parade,
An octopus dons a jolly charade.
"Did you see my treasure? It's shiny and bold!"
"Oh wait, that's just my brother's hair so old!"

Tales of a kraken, or so they say,
But it's just a seal with a kick and a sway.
Hidden beneath are giggles and glee,
In this cove of joy, as wild as the sea!

So bring your snorkel, and don't be shy,
Join the merry dance; we'll laugh till we cry.
In the mysteries lurking, there's fun to explore,
In the cove that holds secrets forevermore!

Where the Sea Meets Silence

Waves whisper jokes to the sand,
Seagulls squawk with a laugh in hand.
Crabs dance sideways, what a sight,
Shells gossip softly, day turns night.

The tide brings treasures, a shoe, a hat,
Driftwood masterpieces, imagine that!
Fish parade in colors so bright,
Their scales reflect the fading light.

The coconut laughs, it's quite a tease,
"Take me home! I'm better than cheese!"
Laughter echoes, creatures in glee,
Frolicking under the palm tree.

With each splash, the secrets unfold,
Stories of pirates, brave and bold.
In this place where the sea does play,
Humor is found in the ocean's spray.

Songs of the Serpent's Nest

A snake with glasses is reading a book,
Nestled in branches where nobody looks.
His laughter ticks, like a clock on a quest,
What is that noise? A worm's silly jest.

The birds join in with a chorus of cheer,
Telling tall tales for all who can hear.
With feathers so bright and voices so clear,
They serenade critters that gather near.

A crab in a tuxedo waltzes the sand,
While turtles on skateboards form a band.
They strum on their shells; it's a wild affair,
Everyone joins in, just try not to stare!

In the nest of the snake, the shenanigans rise,
Nature's pure humor beneath sunny skies.
The laughter grows louder, like waves in a storm,
In this whimsical world, where all is in form.

The Alchemy of Sun and Shell

A sunbeam strikes a curious shell,
Whispers of laughter in its shiny dwell.
The beach is a lab, with sand as the base,
Creating concoctions at a vibrant pace.

The crabs mix cocktails of seaweed delight,
Sipping on bubbles that sparkle so bright.
The starfish take notes from a savvy old ray,
As they all plan a fun beachside ballet.

The waves join in with a dance of their own,
Tickling the toes of the seashell throne.
A sandcastle stands, with a flag on the top,
As the tide rushes in, the party won't stop!

From the depths of the sea to the sun up high,
Secrets are woven where fish and sun fly.
In this magical realm, so quirky and fun,
Every grain of sand tells a tale, one by one.

Heartbeats in Shells and Stones

In a shell, I hear the beats of the sea,
Like a drummer's heart saying, "Come dance with me!"
Stones play maracas, shaking with glee,
Echoes of laughter, wild and carefree.

The seafoam giggles, tickling my toes,
While seaweed sways in a rhythm it knows.
Crustaceans tap-dance on the damp ocean floor,
As the breeze comes along, asking for more.

In this crazy world, where the salt meets the air,
Everything's jolly, nothing's a care.
The clams all sing in a raucous duet,
With a chorus that's catchy, you won't forget!

When night falls down with a starry parade,
The laughter lingers, not even afraid.
For in these rough waters, the joy slips and flows,
Where hearts beat together, and love always grows.

Legends Beneath the Surface

Under waves, a fish with a hat,
Claims to know where the sea cows chat.
He giggles and swims, with a splashy delight,
While crabs share gossip by the moon's soft light.

A turtle named Frank keeps the best tales,
About octopuses who refuse to wear veils.
He dances like jelly with grace and with flair,
But falls on a rock—a grand flop, I declare!

A dolphin appears, with a wink and a flip,
He tells of a treasure, a map on a trip.
But instead of gold, they find old boot laces,
He laughs at their faces, oh, how it amazes!

So if you dive down, where the sea creatures play,
Expect quirky stories to brighten your day.
For beneath the blue, where the laughter is free,
Legends are born from the salt of the sea.

The Silence of the Deep Blue

In the deep blue, where the fish paint the walls,
A crab strums a tune, while a clam answers calls.
A whale plays a song, but it's out of tune,
And seahorses waltz under a bright disco moon.

The octopus, wise, wears glasses and frowns,
As turtles in tuxedos float by with their crowns.
They keep a straight face, while the bubbles just laugh,
Snapping selfies with a very grumpy giraffe.

A sea cucumber dreams of a life on the shore,
Wishing to dance at a fancy seafloor.
With all of this silence, oh what a delight!
The coral boolabas have parties at night!

So when you swim deep, in the hush of the blue,
Look closely for giggles that tickle right through.
For in each quiet corner, a joy will arise,
The sea holds its secrets, but also its sighs.

The Language of Seafoam and Stone

Seafoam whispers secrets, tickling the shore,
While pebbles hold stories from days long before.
A starfish translates with its sparkly sighs,
It cracks a bad joke that brings tears to your eyes.

A sponge in the shallows, so yellow and bright,
Keeps a diary of dreams, well hidden from sight.
The seaweed joins in, with dance moves so bold,
Saying, 'The best part of tides? Always be told!'

The sands tell a tale of a crab with a hat,
Who went on a journey, but got lost in a spat.
The clam didn't help, just kept munching away,
While the whole ocean chuckled at his dismay.

So listen, dear friend, as you stroll by the waves,
For wisdom is shared in the sea's little enclaves.
With laughter and joy in the sprays of the foam,
The tides bring us whispers of far-off homes.

Echoes in the Forgotten Cove

A crab danced a jig on the rocky shore,
While seagulls squawked, wanting more.
A treasure map drawn in invisible ink,
Left all the pirates confused to think.

A fish in a hat gave me a wink,
Said, "Up here, the water's on the brink!"
With a splash and a laugh, they took the plunge,
While I stood back, my humor to indulge.

The tide rolled in with a playful shove,
Rocking my boat like a feathered glove.
But the mermaid laughed, in a shell of gold,
Telling tales of the secrets they hold.

So here in the cove, with laughter and cheer,
Nature whispers, but it's seldom clear.
With every echo, a goofy refrain,
For who wouldn't chuckle while riding a wave train?

Secrets Held by the Waves

The ocean's mouth giggled with salt and foam,
As seashells shared gossip far from home.
"Did you hear about the starfish's dance?
He tripped on a seaweed, lost his chance!"

Dolphins flipped over, catching the breeze,
With tales of crabs and their mad caprices.
"An octopus juggle? What a sight to see!
But he dropped his pearl, oh dear, poor me!"

Waves whispered stories of ships long gone,
Nautical nonsense was their favorite con.
With barnacles chuckling, they settled the score,
While fish threw a party, oh to be four!

So listen closely, let laughter seep,
Among the waves where secrets creep.
For amidst the splash, life's folly reveals,
A joyous world where humor heals.

The Hidden Sanctuary of Coral Dreams

In reefs decorated like a carnival float,
Lived a clam who fancied himself a great goat.
With sea cucumbers as his loyal crew,
They danced in currents, with rhythm so true.

A turtle in shades rolled by with a grin,
Said, "Join us, friend, let the fun begin!"
With jellyfish jelly and seaweed pies,
They served up laughter sprinkled with flies.

The corals were painted in colors so bright,
With whispers of glee as day turned to night.
"Who's the fairest?" cried the fish in the pout,
"I'd say the guy with the bubblegum snout!"

So here in the depths, far from the sun,
Laughter erupts, the merriment's fun.
In a hidden haven where dreams float and play,
Coral's secrets unfold in a whimsical way.

Beneath the Palms' Silent Watch

Under the palms where the coconuts fall,
A parrot pinched pennies and stood tall.
With a squawk he proclaimed, "Treasure awaits!
But first grab some bananas, on fun it predicates!"

A wise old turtle with glasses so thick,
Told tales of a pirate who danced a quick kick.
But when he climbed up, he fell on his face,
"Fear not!" he said, "It's just my grace!"

The pink flamingos laughed, striking a pose,
As crabs played checkers with fraudulent woes.
"Let's roll with the tide," they all cheered aloud,
In this tropical haven, laughter's the crowd.

So next time you wander near rustling leaves,
Listen real close, for the merriment weaves.
Beneath the palms, where the silly ignite,
A comedy of nature brings pure delight!

The Veil of Dusk and Dawn

In twilight's grip, the crabs all dance,
With tiny feet, they take a chance.
The seagulls squawk, they think they're wise,
But miss the fish that hide in disguise.

The sun peeks out, a ball of cheer,
While turtles play their game of smear.
A breeze tickles leaves, they giggle too,
As ocean waves chant a playful boo!

Old shells whisper tales of yore,
Of shipwrecks and pirates, a long-lost lore.
But here, they drape in laughter's glow,
Dancing shadows wherever you go.

As night falls down, the stars will wink,
They know our thoughts before we think.
The moon will chuckle, a fountain of dreams,
In this wild place where laughter beams.

Secrets of the Drifted Anchor

A boat with anchors starts to yawn,
It dreams of waves till the crack of dawn.
The fish laugh hard at the sailor's plight,
While jellyfish swarm like stars at night.

An anchor sits, all rusty and brave,
It tells tall tales of every wave.
With barnacles dressed in polka dots,
Secrets emerge from the fishy plots.

The seaweed giggles, swaying in style,
Its tangled hair adds to the guile.
Whispers bubble up, within the tide,
For who knows what chaos they'll confide?

Yet, in this fun, there's a wink, a nod,
The crab in his shell, feeling like a god.
So let's toast the tales that never get told,
In this playful realm, both silly and bold.

Traces of Old Moons

The moon grins wide, a glowing face,
It pulls the tides, a cosmic chase.
Stars gossip softly about the night,
On shadows that dance, out of sight.

Old lunars tease with a silver beam,
While clams keep secrets, a pearl-filled dream.
Their shells click and clack in the salt-laden air,
What wonders lie deep? A daring affair!

As waves crash down, foam takes a spin,
The laughter of fish is where you begin.
Echoes from nights when the sideshow bloomed,
Are masked by the whispers of seashells zoomed.

A playful breeze wanders, here and there,
Tickling the grass with a cheeky flair.
So join the fun, as the moon starts to glide,
In the realms of magic where giggles reside.

Hidden Reflections in Still Waters

The pond's a mirror, so sly and deep,
Holding secrets that fishy folk keep.
Frogs croak jokes that ripple the glass,
While dragonflies sway, looking like sass.

Reflections bob as the turtles gawk,
At their own faces, they have a shock.
But laughter rings out through the evening haze,
As the water laughs back in its shimmering ways.

Each stone is a throne for the king of the muck,
With grins from the minnows, they'll spin their luck.
Under the lily pads, whispers abound,
Of leafy conspiracies that swirl around.

So let's splash joy in these tranquil spots,
With buddies of bubbles and mismatched knots.
Hidden reflections play games without pause,
Where fun is the rule and laughter the cause.

The Sigh of Forgotten Shores

Upon the sand, the crabs hold court,
In tiny suits, they sharply sport.
They call for fish, they holler loud,
While gulls just chuckle, quite proud.

A turtle laughs, wearing a hat,
Says, "I'm slow, but this is that!"
The sunbeams wiggle, can't behave,
In laughter, echoes roll like waves.

With every tide, the secrets stream,
As seaweed dances, a underwater dream.
The starfish winks, gives a sly cheer,
While seashells gossip, "What's new here?"

So if you wander this sandy place,
Be sure to wear a smile on your face.
The shores whisper tales of joy galore,
As crabs regale on the ocean floor.

Where Shadows Dance with Light

In the twilight glow, shadows play,
Where palm trees offer a cabaret.
The lizards leap, a quirky ballet,
While fireflies join in, come what may.

The sun dips low, and giggles pop,
As coconuts fall with a soft plop.
A whispering breeze joins the fray,
To share secrets in a cheeky way.

Monkeys swing, a merry band,
Trading bananas, quite the grandstand.
Each swing a story, each laugh a sign,
"Come join our party, it's simply divine!"

As night unfolds, the tales ignite,
Beneath twinkling stars, everything feels right.
So pull up a seat, let's all delight,
In the cosmic dance of shadows and light.

The Grotto's Hidden Heart

Deep within the crooked caves,
Where the sea sings and mischief braves.
A clam in pearls thinks it's too grand,
But bubbles burst, yes, isn't life grand?

The sea urchin sips a fizzy drink,
While cave fish gossip, with a wink.
Echoes bounce, as secrets flow,
In this underwater, humble show.

A crab recites poetry in rhyme,
Accompanied by the bubbly chime.
The jellyfish jive, swirl in delight,
Dancing 'til dawn, a magical sight.

So come take a plunge into this spree,
What's hidden deep is joy to see.
The grotto's pulse, alive with mirth,
Reveals sweet laughter, the heart of earth.

Secrets Bloom among the Mangroves

Beneath the boughs, the otters glide,
With a splashy laugh, they turn the tide.
The mangroves murmur, "What's that sound?"
As fish play tag without a bound.

A heron stands, a statue still,
With ambitions grand, it plans a thrill.
But with a slip and quite the fuss,
It almost lands in a waiting bus!

The mudskippers dance a little jig,
Wiggling their tails, feeling quite big.
Muddy cheeks pressed in laughter's spree,
As laughter echoes through the trees.

So roam the roots where mirth entwines,
Among the blossoms, where joy reclines.
For every nook whispers a bright cheer,
In mangrove tales loud enough to hear.

The Enigma of the Silver Lagoon

There's a place where the fish wear hats,
And the crabs dance to the rhythm of spats.
Whispers float on the breeze, they hum,
While turtles moonwalk and call it 'fun'.

Ducks in tuxedos paddle around,
Joking about the sight they have found.
A sunken treasure? Just old flip-flops,
In this quirky lagoon, laughter never stops.

Seagulls sing opera, oh what a sight!
Every splash feels like sheer delight.
"Is that a whale?" someone shouts with glee,
But it's just Flipper, flossing with seaweed!

So come take a dip, leave your worries behind,
In the lagoon where hilarity's defined.
With fish-joined parties and crabby buffets,
You'll remember these moments for all of your days.

Where Time Stands Still

In a place where clocks forget their tick,
The goats wear socks; it's a funny trick.
Mangroves gossip, they share their tales,
About a snail who married two snails.

Coconuts debate on who's the best,
And parrots play chess; they never rest.
The sun shines bright; it's always at noon,
In this timeless realm, life's a cartoon!

Sandcastles build themselves, what a feat!
With seashells as guards, they can't be beat.
Crabs shake hands and offer a toast,
To the moments we cherish and love the most.

So stay for a bit, let laughter ensue,
Where time's just a concept, and so are you.
In this merry land, with antics so silly,
You'll find joy pouring—oh, what a filly!

The Hidden Language of Seashells

Seashells gossip in whispers so sly,
Each colorful spiral holds secrets to pry.
A clam tells stories of oceanic shoo,
While sand dollars giggle at waves passing through.

"Did you hear what the conch said today?"
"It's driving the sand dollars thoroughly cray!"
With each tiny shell, there's a snicker and laugh,
The tide rolls in with its own comic staff.

Starfish are actors on a coral stage,
They perform their antics, a humorous page.
With seaweed sign language, they share a joke,
While crabs chant verses till the waters choke.

So gather your shells, and listen real close,
For the ocean's laughter, you'll surely engross.
From tiny to large, each shell holds a spark,
In the underwater world, it's a party of quark!

Murmurs of the Driftwood Path

On a path made of driftwood, what do we find?
Wise old logs, with tales intertwined.
They grumble about storms, but laugh at the sky,
As pebbles join in, like friends passing by.

Footprints of jellyfish, back and forth sway,
As they reminisce about their last beach day.
"Let's drink some sea foam!" a log starts to cheer,
While starfish on benches share gossip they hear.

Seashells applaud with their tiny little claps,
While the driftwood path giggles through gaps.
A crab in a bowtie recites a short rhyme,
As laughter echoes, eternal in time.

So stroll on this path where humor unravels,
And become part of joy that always travels.
With each step you take, let laughter ignite,
In this whimsical journey, everything's bright!

The Hidden Caverns of Solitude

In a cave where crabs hold court,
A lobster tells jokes, a real sport.
They laugh 'til the seaweed starts to dance,
As clams chime in with a rhythmic prance.

With rock stars like shells, they throw a bash,
Waves crash softly, making quite a splash.
The walls echo giggles, quite a feat,
Just don't ask the sea urchin to compete!

A treasure chest filled with mismatched socks,
Rewards those brave who hack through the rocks.
Mermaids peek in, donning a sly grin,
Their giggles blend with the ocean's din.

So next time you wander where the tide goes,
Look for the cave where chaos flows.
For solitude hides fun finds and cheer,
In the ocean's nooks, you'll want to steer!

Longings Adrift in the Calm

A turtle dreams of a life on land,
But forgets his flip-flops; isn't it grand?
His friends laugh as they swim all around,
While he wonders if sunbathing's profound.

A fish flips by in a polka dot suit,
Declaring, "Chill, it's no time to hoot!"
A seagull quips with a wink in his eye,
"Find me a hammock; let's both have a lie!"

Coconuts roll like wandering fools,
While crabs juggle seashells and tools.
Everyone's longing for some sunny spells,
While sipping on slices of lime and gels.

In the calm, they dream of sandy delights,
Where laughter and joy dance through the nights.
Stuck on that bead in the ocean's vast pool,
They ponder their wishes; the sea is the rule!

The Seabird's Haunting Tale

A seabird perched on a gnarled old tree,
Spins tales of mischief, for all to see.
With feathers of pink and a beak of gold,
He leads ocean critters—so brave and bold!

"Once I stole an ice cream from a whale,
He chased me around, but I swerved without fail.
We raced through the currents, quite the sight,
As fish rolled in giggles, oh what a flight!"

When dusk drapes the sky like a velvet gown,
The seabird dips down, not one to frown.
He dives for his supper—the catch of the day—
Adding laughs to the beach, come join in the fray!

So heed his tales as they flutter and swirl,
In the sea's stories, let laughter unfurl.
For magic resides in every breeze,
In bird's tales of fun, find joy on the seas!

Confessions in the Coral Shadows

In coral-lined corners, the fish convene,
Swapping their secrets, gossip routine.
"I once kissed a crab, oh the horror it brought!"
Laughter erupts—what a twist, what a thought!

A starfish slumps, with a sigh of despair,
"My arms are too short; it's not really fair.
I reach out for snacks but they swim away,
At least I can tickle the turtles in play!"

With bubbles of mirth and tales quite absurd,
The group tells their stories, one after the third.
They spin in the currents, a whirl of delight,
In the shadows of coral, their laughter ignites!

So, swim by their meetings, and don't be a bore,
For what lies in shadows is never a chore.
Join the fish in their funny confessions,
In the depths of the sea, find joy in expressions!

The Haunting of the Twilight Cove

In twilight's glow, the ghostly crew,
Play cards and laugh, but no one knew.
A parrot squawks, 'You owe me rum!'
While old sea shanties make them hum.

The tide rolls in with a cheeky grin,
As pirates dance with tails of fin.
A crab in a hat gives quite a show,
And the moon just beams, 'Oh what a flow!'

Mysterious fog hides tales absurd,
Of mermaids lost and silly birds.
They trade tall tales of treasure to find,
While playfully haunting the unwary mind.

So come along, hear their playful cheer,
In Twilight Cove, where joy's always near.
The laughter's loud, the mishaps grand,
As ghostly mates jive on the sand!

The Journey of Whispering Tides

Sailors set forth where the whispers sing,
With jellyfish dancing, what a silly thing!
A clam tells jokes, or so they say,
While stars flicker on their merry way.

The waves roll high, they giggle and tease,
As turtles wear shades, with just such ease.
The salty breeze plays tricks on minds,
As seagulls giggle, in laughter, they find.

A dolphin flips, and then takes a bow,
To the rhythm of waves, it's pure wow!
Around the bend, the mirthful tide,
With every splash, the worries subside.

So journey where the whispers flow,
Embrace the fun, let your worries go.
In the splash and laughter, you'll find your bliss,
On the waves of joy, you can't miss!

Treasures Beneath the Currents

Beneath the waves, a treasure chest,
Filled with socks from a sea-crew jest!
A fish in a tux named Mr. Finn,
Chortles loud, 'Let the fun begin!'

Crabs wear crowns, and clams spin tales,
Of pirate escapades and goofball fails.
A mermaid's mirror reflects her pout,
'Where's my comb?' she cries, without a doubt!

Pearls with giggles, shiny and round,
As turtles play tag, in silliness found.
The ocean smiles, its secrets known,
In laughter's wake, joy has grown.

So dive for the laughs, not gold or bling,
For underwater fun is the real thing.
Join the dance of the currents so free,
Where every splash is a joke, you see!

The Illusions of Distant Shores

A distant shore with winks and waves,
Where laughter hides in sandy caves.
With flip-flops flying, a race ensues,
As the tide plays tricks, amusing views.

A treasure map with doodles galore,
Points to snacks, and oh, so much more!
A crab chef serves a feast so bright,
With jellybean salad, a true delight!

Mirages dance on the shimmering sea,
One-eyed fish wink, 'Come share with me!'
A coconut cup with a quirky grin,
Bids everyone drink 'til the fun begins!

So roam the shores where laughter's in store,
In the land of giggles, you'll ever explore.
The illusions here are silly yet true,
In distant dreams, let the fun ensue!

Colors of the Dusk-touched Harbor

The sky's a paint spill, oh so bright,
With polka-dots and swirls, a funny sight.
A seagull wears shades, thinks he's so cool,
While fish throw a party, splashing in the pool.

Balloons float by, swaying with the tide,
A crab's got a mustache, quite a strange guide.
The boats wink and giggle, tipsy at best,
Telling tall tales of their day-long quest.

Cheers to the sunset, with giggles galore,
As jellyfish jelly dance on the shore.
With each splash and guffaw, the stars pop out,
These harbor side secrets, we laugh and shout.

So grab a tall drink from the coconut tree,
Join the party, come dance, be so carefree.
As colors swirl on this laughter-filled bay,
In the dusk-touched harbor, let's frolic and play.

The Enchantment of Forgotten Shores

On sandy lanes where lost flip-flops creep,
The crabs weave stories, 'round shadows they leap.
A clam hums a tune, quite out of key,
While sandcastles wobble, just wait and see!

A whispering breeze joins the game of tag,
As seashells click-clack like a cheerful rag.
Mermaids giggle, flipping hair with flair,
Sending seaweed warriors up in the air.

The tide leaves behind a jumbled mess,
With treasures and junk, it's anyone's guess.
A lone starfish juggles, trying to impress,
While sand dunes hold secrets, in loose, funny dress.

So laugh with the waves, let humor convene,
As we prance on shores that aren't always seen.
In forgotten places where magic might pour,
Find joy in the moments, and always explore.

The Dance of Shadows on the Water

Shadows dance lightly on the rippling blue,
Clumsy and happy, such a funny view.
A dolphin does twirls while seabirds can't see,
Their dance moves are fancy – oh, don't you agree?

With splashes of laughter, the waves join the fun,
As turtles with top hats strut under the sun.
Fish throw a disco, but they're all out of sync,
While the seaweeds giggle, oh what do you think?

The moon winks mischievously from above,
Drawing shadows that laugh, as if in true love.
The boats gently sway, gossiping in tow,
To water's own rhythm, they put on a show.

So if you hear chuckles on a moonlit night,
Just know it's the shadows, feeling delight.
Join in their merriment, dance just for fun,
And let the ocean's magic make you feel young.

Secrets Wrapped in Seafoam

Whispers of seafoam curl with delight,
Hiding stories that tickle, laugh all night.
The ocean's a prankster, with shells as its spies,
Sending giggles and bubbles, oh what a surprise!

A message in a bottle - what could it be?
Turns out it's a note from a silly sea flea.
"Dear friend, I'm swimming in jellybean stew,
Bring your best swim trunks, there's fun to pursue!"

A wave tickles toes, then runs off with a grin,
While dolphins hold backfits, wearing fin hats of skin.
The conch shells are laughing, they know it's a joke,
As mermaids just sparkle, puffing out sea smoke.

So dip in the treasure of laughter and fun,
Among seaweed and laughter, let's jump and run.
With secrets so silly, come let's explore,
The magic of surf that makes our hearts soar.

In the Heart of the Atoll

In the heart of the atoll, where the fish wear ties,
Sea turtles dance waltzes under coconut skies.
The crabs throw a party, with a dance floor of sand,
And the seagulls critique, laughing, quite unplanned.

A parrot tells secrets, he squawks with delight,
Exposing the mermaids who swim in the night.
With a splash and a giggle, they swim out of sight,
As all of us wonder what makes them so tight.

The sun sets in colors of pink and of gold,
While jellyfish twirl, with stories untold.
They whisper of treasure buried under the waves,
Yet never quite mention that it's just old graves.

A whispered legend of riches so grand,
Of pirate's lost socks—nobody understands!
Yet here in the atoll, life dances and plays,
With secrets of laughter in the sun's joyous rays.

Tales Carried on Coconut Breezes

Coconut whispers float gently by,
With tales of mischief, oh my, oh my!
The monkeys plot pranks while draped in their fur,
Swapping their hats, oh what a stir!

The waves laugh aloud with a giggly splash,
While crabs tell tall tales in a hurry to dash.
The wind carries chuckles, a symphony sweet,
As sandcastles topple, admitting defeat.

Rumors of pirates, with treasure that's plastic,
Dance with the breeze, oh how fantastic!
A map sketched on a leaf with a scribble so bold,
Leads to all things that could never be sold.

So listen, dear friend, to the breezes that blow,
They'll share every tale if you listen and know.
With laughter and giggles they lighten your day,
In this wonderful world where the funny will play.

The Veiled Portrait of the Lagoon

In the lagoon's embrace, secrets are neat,
With fish in tuxedos, they twirl and they greet.
The octopus paints portraits with colors so bright,
Of a clam holding court in the cool moonlight.

A pelican juggles with fish in the air,
While seaweed gets tangled, in a fashion affair.
The bubbles, they giggle, with chatter and cheer,
As the pirate's lost shoe floats by—a souvenir!

With a wink and a wave, the sea sprites appear,
To dance in the twilight with laughter and cheer.
They'll tickle your toes as you walk by the tide,
Leaving trails of mischief that you cannot hide.

So pull up a chair and let worries drift,
For the lagoon holds treasures, a whimsical gift.
A tapestry woven of laughter and dreams,
Where everyone knows laughter reigns supreme.

Serpentines of the Seafoam

In the seafoam's shimmer, secrets twist and twirl,
With sea snakes in bow ties, they dance and they whirl.
They wink at the sun with a wink of their scales,
As they sing silly songs of the legendary gales.

An octopus chef prepares food with flair,
With seaweed soufflé and barnacle pair.
The starfish plays poker, all laid back in sand,
While the turtles bet just to make things more grand.

The dolphins breakdance, their moves will amaze,
With splashes of laughter in sunlit arrays.
A treasure of giggles lies deep in their eyes,
As they tell of the time a crab won in disguise.

So come join the fun in this nautical jest,
A world of sea secrets, you'll love it the best!
Let the waves carry laughter, let joy be your guide,
In the serpentines of seafoam, together we'll glide.

Sonnet of the Salty Winds

The seagulls squawk, a raucous cheer,
Carrying tales, both far and near.
A crab in a tux, all dressed for the night,
Waltzes on sand, such a curious sight.

The treasures they hide, in shells and in foam,
Wish they could take them, a gypsy to roam.
But alas, they're stuck, on this sun-kissed shore,
Trading old stories, always wanting more.

Under the sun, the drinks overflow,
Lime and coconut, put on a show.
Dancing with laughter, the waves join in,
As the palm trees sway, with mischief and grin.

So raise your glass to the whimsy at hand,
For the salty winds rule this lively land.
Secrets aplenty, all wrapped up in jest,
The fun never ends, here we are truly blessed.

A Reverie of Endless Horizons

Stars twinkle bright, like fireflies at play,
On this vast expanse, we laugh and sway.
A dolphin jumps high, wearing a grin,
Hoping to join in, where the fun has been.

A hammock swings low, 'neath a coconut tree,
While parrots gossip, as loud as can be.
"Did you see that flip?" "What a splash!" they say,
While the sunset paints gold, at the close of the day.

The sun dips low, as the laughter erupts,
Ice cream melts fast, like sandcastle dumps.
Splashes of color, a painter's delight,
We chase all our worries, 'til the stars are in sight.

So let's build a sandman, with shells for a tie,
And crown him with seaweed, watch laughter fly.
For in this realm, where the fun never ends,
Endless horizons are where laughter transcends.

The Keeper of the Tides' Story

At the water's edge, a tale begins,
With shells as the pages, laughter the wins.
The octopus paints, with colors so bright,
A masterpiece done, by the ebb and the light.

The turtles all gather, with winks and a nod,
To share all the gossip, it's fabulously odd.
"Did you hear what the fish said about the sea hog?
He danced like a man, in a thick, furry fog."

The tide rolls in, with mystery and charm,
But keeps all its secrets, safe from alarm.
With giggles and splashes, they blend with the night,
The waves sing their stories, beneath starlit height.

So come, gather 'round, let the charades commence,
In this watery theater, with laughs immense.
For the keeper of tales has nothing but cheer,
Where the ocean's embrace feels like home every year.

Veils of Mist upon the Rocks

A fog rolls in, with a wink and a laugh,
Hiding the treasures of the old and the daft.
"Did you find my shoe?" calls out a brave bear,
As the mist dances swirls, without a single care.

The pelicans plunge, with comedic flair,
Scaring up fish, while they leap in the air.
And jokes are exchanged, like conch shells divine,
Each secret they share, paired with tropical wine.

At dawn, the sun breaks through, peeking shy,
Casting shadows that stretch, as the gulls glide by.
With each sip of brilliance, the humor ignites,
For the waves tickle shores, through fun-filled nights.

So lift your spirits high, in a toast to the mist,
Where laughter and secrets seem impossible to resist.
For all those who wander, a hearty cheer shouts,
To the veils of enchantment, what life is about!

Beneath the Banyan's Embrace

Beneath the banyan, a parrot sneezed,
It startled a crab, who danced, quite pleased.
A monkey swung by, with a laugh in its eyes,
While coconuts fell, to everyone's surprise.

The sun shined down, a warm glowing light,
As tourists came by, in shorts way too tight.
They tripped on their sandals, while chasing a breeze,
And slipped on a mango, oh what a tease!

A turtle just chuckled, from under the shade,
At the sight of a kid, in a colorful braid.
He offered his shell, as a surfboard that's grand,
But all he got back was a cold, sandy hand.

So, if you're in trouble, and falling apart,
Just sit by the banyan, let laughter restart.
For the craziest tales, and the best of the fun,
Are waiting beneath, when the day's nearly done.

The Twilight of Lost Horizons

As dusk rolled in, with a blush and a sigh,
A fish told a joke, to a gull flying by.
But the gull just replied, with a flap of his wings,
'You're only funny when a seaweed sings!'

Under the twilight, the waves played along,
A crab grabbed a shell, and sung a soft song.
He danced on the shore, filled with joy and glee,
While a shy little starfish pretended to flee.

A sailor appeared, with a wink in his eye,
Holding a treasure — a pie made of sky.
He offered a slice, to the fish and the bird,
But they laughed and they said, 'That's absurd!'

Yet twilight can hold, the best of our nights,
With tales of the sea, full of funny delights.
So gather your friends, and let laughter grow,
For the secrets of twilight are the best, don't you know?

Secrets of the Driftwood Path

Along the driftwood path, a seal waved its paw,
To a clam who just sat, in a most awkward flaw.
He shouted, 'Hey friend! Come and join the parade!'
But the clam simply blinked, like he couldn't evade.

Then came a whole group, of sand crabs in line,
With tiny top hats and a sweet bottle of brine.
They taught all the seaweed a dance on the sand,
While shells all around gave a heartfelt hand.

A hermit crab shouted, 'This party's for real!'
With snacks served in shells, they all started to squeal.
When a breeze came along, whispering so light,
They twirled and they spun, till the end of the night.

So if you feel dull, or lost in your day,
Just wander the driftwood, let merriment sway.
For laughter is hidden, where secrets reside,
In the shells and the sand, let your heart be your guide.

Whispers of the Sea's Heart

The sea's heart does whisper, with bubbles and laughs,
As fishermen row with their wobbly crafts.
A jellyfish giggled, with arms all aglow,
'Trying to catch fish? Well, good luck, though!'

A dolphin chimed in, with a leap and a flip,
'You should wear your goggles, or risk a bad trip!'
But the fishermen grinned, as they splashed and they poked,
'We'd rather make friends, than be fried or be soaked!'

So waves threw parties, with clam shells as chairs,
While sea turtles danced, despite their slow stares.
They cheered for the night, with a heartwarming cheer,
As the moon watched above, its magic so clear.

And if you should wander, where laughter holds fast,
In the whispers of waves, let your worries drift past.
For the sea holds the secrets of joy in its art,
And the best of its treasures lie deep in its heart.

The Floating Lorekeepers

There once were some fish who could chat,
They shared all the news from their mat.
With a wiggle and splash,
They'd gossip and dash,
While a crab played the role of a brat.

A turtle with glasses looked wise,
Said, 'Underwater, no need for disguise!'
But the octopus, sly,
Gave a wink and a cry,
'Just wait till the laughter arrives!'

The bubbles they blew formed a tale,
Of a clam who once danced on a whale.
With every funny twist,
You could hardly resist,
To believe in their whimsical scale.

So if you should float on this scene,
Watch out for the fish and their sheen.
With a chuckle and cheer,
You'll find laughter here,
In the antics of those who are keen.

Ghosts of the Coral Gardens

In a garden where corals do bloom,
Lurk the ghosts with a soft, spooky gloom.
They peek from their shells,
With giggles and yells,
While performing their underwater zoom.

One ghost made a spell with some sand,
To conjure up jokes that were grand.
With a flare and a jump,
He'd make everyone thump,
As they chuckled and danced hand in hand.

A seahorse joined in with great flair,
Who pranced like ballet was rare.
'This ghost is no fright,
Just a laugh in the night,
When all of the critters declare!'

So should you find yourself down below,
With the ghostly brigade in tow.
Just remember to grin,
Join the fun, spin and spin,
For the sea is a place for a show!

Beneath the Sailor's Song

In a tavern by the coast, you will find,
A sailor with tales that are blind.
With each pint he pours,
He shares silly scores,
Of adventures that twist in your mind.

He swears that a mermaid passed through,
With a hat made of seaweed and glue.
She winked and did twirl,
And gave him a whirl,
Leaving fish fry and laughter in view.

He boasts of a fish that could sing,
A sea bass with quite the bling-bling.
With a jig and a laugh,
It diverts the whole staff,
And inspires the crowd to join in.

So next time you hear a sailor's tune,
Laugh along, let your heart be in bloom.
For the beat of the sea,
And the joy that will be,
Holds a magic that brightens the room.

Echoes of Forgotten Marinas

In a marina where boats used to sway,
Lives a seagull with stories to play.
She dances on masts,
And tells tales of the past,
While the fish roll their eyes in dismay.

One tale speaks of a sailor quite bold,
Who traded his boots for a mold.
With an anchor for flair,
He sailed through the air,
Causing chaos of laughter untold.

The barnacles chuckle in glee,
As the waves form a giggling spree.
With a trot and a shuffle,
The water does ruffle,
Echoes carry their fun to the sea.

So if you should walk by the pier,
And catch whispers that tickle your ear,
Join in the fun,
Let your laughter run,
For the secrets of joy float right here!

www.ingramcontent.com/pod-product-compliance
Lightning Source LLC
Chambersburg PA
CBHW072219070526
44585CB00015B/1413